Codependency Workbook

7 Steps to Break Free from People Pleasing, Fear of Abandonment, Jealousy, and Anxiety in Relationships

Rita Hayes

losses, direct or indirect, that are incurred as a result of the use of the information contained within this document, including, but not limited to, errors, omissions, or inaccuracies.

Table of Contents

Introduction

When you grow up in a dysfunctional home, you learn to be ignorant to your self. You learn to run away from unpleasant feelings and emotions. You learn to betray yourself and your needs. As you grow older, it becomes more arduous to confront these emotions and problems as they accumulate. You develop an addiction to ruinous coping mechanisms, be it drugs, alcohol, relationships, approval, or needing to be needed— because the only way you know how to feel love is when you perform for it. Because the more taxing it feels to dishonor your needs, the more you indulge in the coping mechanisms that only help you to keep your face above the water—while everything you're running away from anchors you from beneath. Whenever you became visibly upset as a child, your parent or guardian would glare at you to "fix your face." You were forced to painfully swallow that lump of anger and sadness. It happened so often that; eventually, suppressing difficult emotions became instinctive. And even now, as you are aware of this learned instinct, you can't seem to be able to turn it off. It's frustrating. But at least you know what's wrong, and that's a good start.

You know that you've been a victim in some shape or form, and you either build up resentment towards those who victimized you or towards yourself. They're the ones who made you feel incredibly alone for as long as you can remember. And now you'll do anything you can to not feel alone, or at least to forget that that's how you feel. Your resentment keeps you in this loop where victimizing yourself becomes an intricate part of your identity. It's how you enable your destructive habits, and how you enable others to take advantage of you. This cycle continues, constantly reaching full circle until it's all you know. Until it's all that's familiar, and anything outside of all that you know outside of that cycle is so terrifying and inconceivable. This is why the circle needs to break. And this is the book that will help you do it.

Imagine a circle of preschoolers playing the game of "Pass The Potato" on the school field, standing in a circle. A new kid comes to join them, so what do they do? They break the circle to make it bigger so that the newcomer has their own space, and the circle is not the same again. In the same way, when we choose to allow a new perspective into our minds, the way we view the world and ourselves widens. However, destructive mental loops are much harder to break. They need to be stretched continuously and consistently. At times it will feel as though you are making progress, only to feel like you've gone right back to square one. The reality of personally trying to recondition your mind is that it will put up a fight because you're forcing it to think differently and to let go of the thought patterns with which it has become familiar. That's why you need to be aware of your toxic mental loops and accept that they exist. Admitting to self-betrayal can garner much denial, especially when we realize that as we try to protect ourselves, we may have unnecessarily hurt those that are close to us. It's why we need to be willing to be brutally honest with ourselves. No, do not talk down on yourself. Be honest but leave room for your humanness. The best and worst parts of yourself—and everything in between—can coexist.

Betraying yourself can manifest in the form—and to whatever degree—of "people-pleasing," "fear of abandonment," 'jealousy,' or "relationship anxiety" or some combination of these states of being. These are the destructive attributes that we will be looking at in the following chapters. They may overlap and even stem from one source, and each trait might reveal itself within you in different situations for different reasons. It may help to single each destructive trait out and deal with it individually. However, dealing with one might also partially mediate the others.

What might make being able to recognize your detrimental thought patterns difficult is spending most of your time in environments that feed into your toxic traits. Such as places where we feel the need to perform extensively to be somewhat acknowledged. And sometimes, even when we're aware that these environments function at our expense, we remain in them and survive off of distractions. And sometimes, that's all we can do because it's how we remain safe. However, for the sake of your sanity, do yourself a favor and try to stay grounded. Pull yourself out of your victim mentality. Sometimes staying in the victim mentality is easier because it means we don't have to take responsibility for how we think, how we feel, and how we act. Know that your anger and pain at those you love isn't unfair to them, no matter how much they might have also gone through. However, that pain and anger are not an excuse to remain complacent. They are reason enough for you to stay present and to let go of the anchors that pull you down and keep you drowning. This doesn't mean rigorously analyzing every thought that passes your mind or your behaviors. A great deal of overcoming your destructive attributes requires you to experience the discomfort of feeling the emotions you've suppressed. Your body can deal with this discomfort in a number of ways; you just have to remember to allow it.

If you have put yourself in a position when perhaps you used your pain as an excuse to hurt yourself or others, this book will help you realize that even if that's the case, you still deserve redemption. You deserve to want it for yourself. However, you will also come to understand that being the victim of a situation that led to your self-deprecating path does not make you the good guy. As people are entitled to their opinions of you, you can end up being the one who tries to manipulate them into thinking whatever you want them to think about you. The following chapters will illuminate the various ways in which your body may process your suppressed emotions. They will also demonstrate how to deal with each toxic trait in a detailed step-by-step process. So if you know, you're ready to face yourself, and if you're prepared to get called out, then come with me.

Chapter 1:

People Pleasing

The minds of children are often likened to sponges, which means that they are exceedingly impressionable. They are more likely to be easily shaped by outside factors. An example of this could be observations noted by Fernandez and Smith-Cairns (2018) in a study central to language acquisition in children. They argue that children have the ability to extract and tell apart the prosodic pattern of their mother tongue from other languages in *utero* and as neonates (babies four weeks or younger). Carroll (2007) argues that children seem to only gain self-awareness from the age of four years old as they begin to develop their "episodic memory" (memories of experiences from a subjective point of view). However, everything they've learned until then, be it behaviors or thought patterns, still remains a part of their knowledge of their world. Carroll (2007) also cites Piaget (1962), who studied object permanence in children, and one of the skills that children developed, which indicated their acquisition of object permanence, was "deferred imitation." Deferred imitation is when a child imitates a behavior that it has seen before. If we take all these observations into account, we can conclude that behaviors such as people-pleasing are learned in homes where children were expected to handle responsibilities and situations they were not ready for. However, people-pleasing does not always stem from childhood experiences. In some cases, individuals learn to people-please in adulthood. This may be a result of not being sufficiently educated on the harsh reality that the world can make you feel small and insignificant. Even supportive homes can set you up for destruction when they don't equip you with the tools to deal with people who come off as intimidating, bitter, or narcissistic. You end up being at their mercy, feeling obligated to attain their approval. They will breadcrumb you to make sure that you keep coming back, and barely feed your developing addiction to being needed, basically grooming you into codependency. Another detrimental aspect of people-pleasing is that it doesn't only extend to those who teach it to you, but also to those who see an opportunity to use you. This is why having strong values is essential. They keep you grounded.

According to Martin (2016), people-pleasing is a "combination of thoughts and behaviors" exhibited by individuals who will go to extremes to please others, often at their own expense. Some are often led by the belief that by virtue of being a good person, the world owes it to them to return that goodness. Hence, they will overextend themselves in order to receive that goodness multiplied. Others go out of their way to appear harmless and useful. They are also led by the same belief, however, they think that not expecting that goodness in return, makes them better people and more deserving of it. They'll never express this outwardly, even as they overextend themselves as well. This 'goodness' often goes unreturned, even after it has garnered the approval that they craved so much. This upsets them, but they never want to ruin the image and reputation that they've built for themselves, and so they internalize those emotions. They build up their resentment for the world. Martin (2016) also notes that people-pleasers have a hard time saying "No." It seems that along the line, these individuals either forget or disregard their agency in their own choices in an effort to blend in, or again, seem harmless. Acting this way is what they feel keeps them safe from rejection or abandonment. But it also keeps them from being themselves. People-pleasers also worry about what others think of them (Martin, 2016), and this leads to them internalizing all external validation and invalidation. They rely on how other people identify them for their sense of self. Most of the time it seems that they can't really differentiate between the kind of feedback that is safe for them to internalize and the feedback that isn't. Perhaps this can be attributed to the possibility that they're not fully aware of their internalization. This is dangerous because already they have dishonored their needs and desires, the very traits that spell out their sense of self.

Martin (2016) argues that people-pleasers carry an overwhelming amount of fear. They fear disappointing those whose approval they seek, they fear being rejected, they fear their own anger. They go to great lengths to appear passive, such as choosing to never voice their opinions or to disagree. They may have learned this as children, where their parents would give them the silent treatment if, for example, they expressed an opinion that displeases the parent. Consider the following scenario:

Mom: Aiden, eat your food now!

Aiden: But mommy, I don't like mashed potatoes.

Mom: I will tell you one last time, Aiden. Finish that plate.

Aiden: (*stares at Mom's angry face with glassy eyes.*)

Mom: Fine. (Gets up from the table and starts with the dishes.)

Aiden: (*tries to eat the mashed potatoes and fails miserably. He gets up from his table and leaves his plate next to the pile of dishes that mom is washing. She doesn't acknowledge him*). Mommy, your hair looks nice today. (*Mom stays silent*). I liked the chicken you made me for lunch. (*Mom stays silent*).

Let's assume that Aiden is six years old. From this scenario alone we can conclude that because of Mom's actions, Aiden feels responsible for Mom's emotions, which couldn't be farther from the truth. What he understands is that mom is upset because he won't eat his mashed potatoes, when in reality, we could say that mom is upset because Aiden won't listen to her. Whether Aiden is able to understand both of these subjective perceptions or not becomes irrelevant because as he tries to soften Mom up with his compliments, he ultimately learns that he always needs to try and make her happy or simply not angry. This is to avoid feeling rejected or emotionally abandoned. He now understands that this is how you keep the ones you love around you, even if it means betraying yourself. Even if it means dishonoring who you are. This is where Aiden, and so many others, learn to people-please.

Martin (2016) states that people-pleasers carry a great deal of resentment because they do things out of obligation rather than out of genuine desire. When you spend too much time doing things for other people while you worry about how they might receive your efforts or you, there is very little room for worrying about yourself. And in that space, all you can do is rest because you're so tired. You secretly wish that people felt sorry for you and took the time to take care of you too. But as a people-pleaser, you won't let yourself express your needs. Spending most of your life psychoanalyzing those around you doesn't mean that that effort is guaranteed to be reciprocated. People cannot—and will not—read your mind. When people-pleasers stay quiet about what they want, those wants turn into expectations—and when those expectations aren't met—they become resentful. It's easier to blame the world when you fail to take responsibility for taking care of yourself. Perhaps when a part of you wasn't nurtured as a child by your primary caregivers, who scared you into never placing any blame on them for the hurt that they inflicted, you feel forced to find an alternative for that blame. You either direct it at yourself to avoid conflict, or you act out, directing it at the world. People-pleasers also try to avoid conflict at all costs, especially on their own. They often feel unsafe to express their true feelings, as conflict exacerbates their fears of rejection, being unlovable, or unworthy (Martin, 2016). So staying quiet and passive becomes a defense mechanism. This may be a result of witnessing or being part of conflicts that escalated quickly and dangerously.

People-pleasing is an acquired state of being, whether in adulthood or in childhood. The people who live their lives this way identify strongly with the benefits that come with being a people-pleaser, which are often outweighed by the costs. They view themselves as victims, but on the contrary, they can be just as manipulative as the narcissists, which keeps them in an unhealthy cycle of self-deprecation. People-pleasers are yet to understand that no matter what they do to "keep the peace," those that perceive them are entitled to their opinions of them. They may be, in essence, good people. But they are also capable of being incredibly spiteful and manipulative, like Mom in the previously demonstrated scenario. They don't want to accept that they are capable of harm. If we can backtrack and analyze the situation further, we can conclude that Mom's silent treatment is a reaction to not being seen as a good mom for trying to get her child to eat healthily. She takes serious offense to Aiden overlooking this image she is trying to project to him. We can further conclude that Mom is a codependent people-pleaser, grooming her son to exhibit the same traits. She illuminates the ugly side of people-pleasing and codependency. It is worth mentioning that people-pleasers fear being seen as bad people. Like Mom, they will justify their spitefulness by victimizing themselves and forcing others to take responsibility for their emotions. Through Aiden, the cycle continues.

How Do We Overcome This?

1: Admit It.

You have to stop being afraid of yourself. You are not the shame, or the guilt or the anger, or the pain that you harbor inside. These are the parts of you that you need to learn to love. The parts whose existence you need to accept before you can let go. Martin (2016) has argued that people-pleasers develop the tendency to minimize or deny their feelings. The problem with this is you convince your mind that your feelings are insignificant, but your body will beg to differ. You may feel a weighty tightness in your chest, the more you deny yourself the right to feel. At its worst, this is a form of self-dehumanizing because feeling is human. You need to internalize the fact that you are not the best or worst parts of yourself; those are your attributes. People-pleasing is one of the few ways an unhealed wound can manifest because the coexistence of your worst and best parts within you can be messy. It becomes messier when you are not curious about yourself. The most challenging step when overcoming a form of codependency such as people-pleasing is admitting and accepting that you have been a people-pleaser. As aforementioned, this can garner much denial. Be willing to recognize and acknowledge those ugly feelings you have buried deep within because you are about to get to work. You are about to excavate all of that muck out of you. You are about to begin rehabilitating yourself.

Your mind and your heart will resist, making you feel guilty. You will feel the resistance in your body, but do not allow this to discourage you. As a people-pleaser, you would have looked at the world through rose-colored glasses. This means that you would have confused kindness with niceness. Make an effort to take these glasses off. Whenever people decided for you that your priorities could be rescheduled, I know you felt a surge of emotion bubble up in your chest. I also know that after a while, you couldn't identify this emotion because a part of you refused to see that blatant crossing of boundaries for what it was: Disrespect. You have been treated with disrespect, and once you allow yourself to see that, you will become angry. Very angry. You will be upset with those who consistently disregarded your well-being and your priorities for only their benefit. You might also be angry with yourself for letting it happen for so long. You won't be afraid of your anger anymore, but be careful not to let this emotion overwhelm you.

You also have to allow yourself to cry. I don't mean suppressed sobs and tearful eyes. I'm telling you that you need to release those suppressed sobs into audible cries. Allow yourself to cry for as long as you need to. You will feel lighter, and you will feel your body thanking you. But remember that this is only the beginning

2: Recognize That You Have a Choice.

You may have been a victim, but that does not mean that you have always been innocent. You might still be in denial and find being a people-pleaser to be inconceivable. Don't worry, you won't understand it all at once, so take all the time you need. This might be caused by the fact that people-pleasers tend not to understand the concept of being used, and in that sense, they can't see past themselves. Don't be afraid to see yourself in a position where you are the one dealing the harm. Accept that you are capable of being harmful, but know that you can choose not to be. Once you've accepted that, then you might be able to understand how you were taken advantage of, what that cost you, how you reacted, and how you might have affected other people in your reaction. You will understand why allowing yourself to be angry is actually one of the most notable markers of who you are.

"No," is a complete sentence. You're allowed to say it. Say it as many times as you see fit. Say it even as your voice cracks, but also **mean** it. You can expect some resistance from yourself here, coming in the form of shame or guilt. You don't have to react to these emotions, but you can acknowledge them—and you can trust that they will always reveal something about you that needs to be addressed. Unless you are tired, if your emotions cause you to halt, it is not an indication that you need to stop investigating, which is why you need to think about why they've arisen. If the reason is initially unclear, then you need to keep going until you reach the root source of the problem. Part of what makes it hard to say "No," for a people-pleaser is that they believe they are responsible for triggering the unpleasant emotions in other people. They are also made to think that they are the ones who have to "make it better" by changing those unpleasant emotions into happy ones. Little do they know that how other people react to you expressing yourself says more about them than it does about you. Choose to be honest about how you feel, no matter how they react. But you don't have to start there. You can start by stalling. It is perfectly okay to tell them you'll think about it and give yourself the permission to do so. And if you still say no after that, you have NOT wasted anybody's time. If anything, they're the ones who have no respect for your time or your priorities.

People-pleasers often operate on what I'd like to term as the "I have to"-basis. You're constantly pasting those three words in front of every request thrown at you. As previously stated, people-pleasers have a sense of obligation to tend to the needs of others more than their own. Think of the "I have to"-basis as a parameter in your mind, and you can switch it on or off based on how it affects your priorities first. Then you can decide on whether you *have* to do something, either for yourself or someone else, or not. Know that you don't *have* to subscribe to other people's needs all the time or too limiting beliefs. You don't have to go where you don't want to or listen to someone else's opinions of you. Knowing that you don't *have to* is a liberating belief. It provides you with a protective layer that, unless you indulge, keeps you from internalizing the limiting beliefs that the world imposes on you.

3: Use Your Discernment.

Doing this work will eventually lead to you becoming more self-aware and intuitive, but it won't happen immediately. You may find yourself reverting back to the habits that kept you in a people-pleasing cycle, and when this happens, please handle yourself with compassion. Discern whether you are slipping back because you miss the familiarity of your old cycle. If this is the case, accept that that's how you feel, and know that it doesn't make you weak, nor does it render the work you've done null or insignificant. Part of it is keeping yourself in check, so if you detect that you're enabling destructive behavior again, then you're still making good progress.

You are human, after all. The thing about ruinous learned behaviors is that when you repeatedly exhibit them, they become automatic, which means that not much thought goes into them. And so, trying to unlearn them requires you to pay attention to the thought patterns and the behaviors that follow subconsciously. Consider the contexts in which they always appear and the role you play. Ask yourself if the role suits you, and if not, change it.

Chapter 2:

Fear of Abandonment

The term "fear of abandonment" is often loosely included when people speak about the forms in which codependency comes. When we hear it, we may think of it as generally being afraid of being left behind, or being afraid of being forgotten, or immediately how it might subjectively apply to us and our lives. And perhaps having this fear, while it may stem from a common source, is somewhat unique to each individual who experiences and acts from it. Those who have self-sabotaging habits are often frowned upon in the world, especially if they act outwardly. However, self-sabotaging habits can be just as undetectable and subtle, and perhaps we all harbor them subconsciously. Like people-pleasing, self-sabotaging behaviors and thought patterns are learned because, at one point, it made sense to employ them. Do you ever wonder why you feel like you are struggling to connect with someone? Your intuition will tell you that there is a blockage. Maybe it will feel like you keep circling around each other, and the circle doesn't get smaller or bigger. It remains precisely the same, but that's what makes it frustrating. Does this dynamic sound familiar?

Cuppen (2019) illustrates the fear of abandonment by dividing it into two conjoined parts: *Separation anxiety* (fear of abandonment) and *fear of attachment* (fear of bonding). She states that these parts are two sides of the same coin and coexist in a powerful dynamic (a force field-like connection). Cuppen (2019) argues that the "dynamic is inside you," which implies that you could either be on the side of separation anxiety or the fear of attachment, and each side is complex. The sides are polar opposites, which means it's an either/or situation. It is impossible to operate from both separation anxiety and fear of attachment simultaneously. That's why you will find that people with separation anxiety are attracted to people with a fear of attachment and vice versa, whether it is platonic or romantic. There is a deep fear of losing love at play that causes those who live with this fear to create a "safe distance" between themselves and the ones they love. It is like an unspoken boundary, and it protects them from being in a space that forces them to be vulnerable. However, if either of them—separation anxiety holder and the fear of attachment holder—crosses this boundary, the relationship loses balance as it was already doomed from the start.

Separation Anxiety and Fear of Attachment

Imagine growing up in a home where you never really formed a close bond with whomever was looking after you. As a child, you're not yet conscious of your emotional development, especially when no one is investing in your emotional intelligence. This is because you haven't yet developed self-awareness, so this doesn't really bother your young mind until you grow old enough to start forming your own thoughts and opinions about how you personally see and experience the world. You quickly understand that when it comes to dealing with intense emotions, you're on your own and it's hard because you are clueless. Feeling clueless about something that's going on within you can be terrifying, and being terrified often triggers a quick response—or a defense mechanism—that will quickly (and temporarily) avert the fear somehow before it takes control. You could either minimize your emotions by trying to convince yourself that it's not a big deal, you might be harsh with yourself by denying your feelings and telling yourself that you shouldn't be feeling them or might acknowledge your emotions, but because you don't know how to deal with them, you suppress them. Abandoning yourself becomes your dynamic as you grow older. Along comes a new friend who is genuinely concerned about your feelings, and genuinely curious about who you are. Having grown up in an environment that forced you to develop a defense mechanism whenever you felt something unpleasant, you've led yourself to a point where you will not be able to immediately identify your deepest desires—such as deep intimacy.

When you and your friend need to go to separate locations during the holidays, you find yourself falling into a depressive state. All you can think about is how much you miss them, and it upsets you. You're either cantankerous or crying constantly at the thought of not being together at that very moment. It upsets you when they're not immediately available to reassure you that they care about you. Sound familiar? What you're experiencing is separation anxiety. Cuppen (2019) has argued that the dynamic created by the fear of abandonment develops subconsciously, so you won't be immediately aware of it when it affects you, especially if you'd never experienced intimacy before. However, the intensity of your emotions may be confusing and daunting. Unfortunately, this will only fuel your separation anxiety, if you are not already aware of, or doing something about it.

Cuppen (2019) notes that when you're a person with separation anxiety, you will find yourself being frightfully focused on your friend or partner, and you will feel the need to cling on or hold on to them. You will constantly yearn for closeness with them, need constant reassurance about their feelings for you, or their commitment to you. A part of you recognizes their need for deep intimacy as well. This is part of why people with separation anxiety and people with a fear of attachment are attracted to each other; they mirror each other this way. And while there is nothing wrong with asking for reassurance, a constant need for it may be a cause for concern. If this is a pattern for you in your relationships, you may need to examine your patterns and behaviors in them.

People with a fear of attachment need—and crave—intimacy in the same way that those with separation anxiety do, except they view it as more of a security risk. Cuppen (2019) notes that the people who fear bonding with others and those with separation anxiety will circle around each other, and this is what keeps the risk of their fears from being realized. However, it is also what keeps them from forming a strong authentic bond with each other. Whenever they start feeling what Cuppen (2019) terms as the "hidden claim,"—which is the deep subconscious need to cling to your partner or friend, often exhibited and expected by the person with separation anxiety—they will distance themselves more, become aloof and emotionally distant. This will fuel the other party's hidden claim, even if they are treated with disrespect until they eventually let go of the person with the fear of attachment. The most heartbreaking part is that you recognize each other's needs because they are one and the same, but you are too afraid to meet each other in the middle.

Where Could It Stem From?

Cuppen (2019) illustrates the early stages of a healthily developing bond between a mother and her newborn child, called "Healthy Symbiosis." She notes that for healthy development, a child needs to experience belonging, warmth, love, and security. As the baby enters into symbiosis with its mother, it is necessary that these needs are fulfilled so that the child feels welcome and safe as it arrives in the world. Furthermore, the trust that is established through symbiosis allows for the child to strive for independence because he/she trusts that he/she is supported by their parent. In this scenario, the parent does not project their unmet needs on their child, and this establishes a reliable foundation of security and trust where the child feels confident in pursuing relationships on his/her own. When healthy symbiosis is disrupted, the child will experience abandonment in some form or another. The parent or caregiver—for whatever reason, knowingly or unknowingly—prioritizes their own unmet needs over the child's, and instead of the child having to experience warmth and security for healthy symbiosis, its first experience of the world is abandonment. Abandonment can be emotional and/or physical, and ultimately, underneath separation anxiety and fear of attachment are deep abandonment wounds that stem from negligent or unavailable primary caregivers. Either a parent too busy dealing with their own repressed trauma to be emotionally available for their child, prolonged periods (divorce/trips/simply walking in and/or out of the child's life) spent apart, or not receiving enough physical affection as a child (Cuppen, 2019, p. 3).

The children whose emotional growth develops within a disrupted symbiotic bond are affected in quite a few ways, as they become familiar with a lack of security from a young age, even before they have their sense of self. Their feelings of panic, protest, and anger at the thought of losing the person they intuitively know is meant to be their caregiver, have to be thwarted in the event that they sense the threat of abandonment. The development of their self-awareness is stunted. Moreover, as they grow, they become more attuned to their parents' (primarily their mother's) emotions than their own; this behavior extends to the relationships they form outside of parental or familial ties. This is what Cuppen (2019) terms as "Entangled Symbiosis," where children can even develop a certain loyalty towards their caregivers and feel responsible for making sure that their parent does not feel abandoned. As Cuppen (2019) notes, these individuals grow up to be highly sensitive people with a tremendous capacity for empathy. However, they struggle to separate their own emotions from the external influx of emotions that they absorb from others.

People with separation anxiety understand that they need to be vulnerable in order to truly connect with a person, but once they allow themselves to be, they can get carried away. When this happens, they bore a sinkhole into the relationship in which they either face their abandonment wounds or distract themselves heavily. They are often left alone in this sinkhole, as the one who fears to bond with them moves further away from them. When you've relied on how someone treats you as an anchor for your identity, you risk the world falling beneath your feet when that anchor starts to pull away from the ground. You risk never knowing who you are and how to be you. Your sense of self will be severely affected because in your tremendous need to be reassured or needed, you find yourself strongly identifying your worth with how your friend or partner responds to that need. Underneath the fear of attachment is often a great deal of self-loathing. You might even question your right to exist. You feel unworthy of love and emotional stability, and even though deep down you understand that it is your desire, you reject it because your self-loathing outweighs your desires. It sounds inconceivable, but it's possible to feel this way. It's easier to accept abandonment when you think you deserve it. Cuppen (2019) notes that when people with a fear of attachment distance themselves if they are being called to be vulnerable in their relationships. They justify this by choosing to view their friends or partner(s) as "not good enough,"—projecting their own insecurities onto them.

What Do We Do About It?

1: Instead, Turn Around and Walk Inwards With Compassion.

In Physical Theatre, it is believed that the body is a "writing place" from the inside, and that the body has a logic of its own (Oyěwùmí, 2005). Cuppen (2019) notes that the body can physically reflect the loneliness and emptiness caused by an abandonment wound where the muscle tension decreases, the shoulders slump as if the spine is struggling to keep them upright, and the legs become weak. Cuppen's (2019) observations and Oyěwùmí's (2005) argument imply that we are not in control of how our bodies reflect our internal experiences. Perhaps our bodies only begin to reflect our internal experiences when we harbor unpleasant emotions. Because you are so attuned to the physical/emotional needs of others, you are out of touch with your own. Therefore, start by coming back to your body. Lay down on the ground somewhere you feel safe. Allow the trauma to resurface from within. Learn to listen to your body and feel where the emotions are sitting in it. When you do, you're likely to feel scared, and you'll stop yourself from allowing those heavy feelings to leave. By now, you would have built up inhibitors for when you feel your emotions physically. Pay attention to each time you feel your inhibitors blocking you from feeling, and then start over. When you start over, ease yourself into the discomfort. Allow your body the autonomy to react however it needs to, whether your limbs start trembling, or if you need to curl up into a ball. If you feel yourself on the brink of a panic attack, consider having someone you feel completely safe with there with you, and seek professional help.

Accept that you don't know who you are, but know that you *have to* take full agency in deciding what your identity looks like. Being out of touch with your needs and desires will do that to you. Know that your identity won't be set in stone, and allow it to be fluid. I'd like to think that there is more power and safety in knowing something than in believing it, although both states of being come hand-in-hand. Knowledge grounds you, belief exalts the knowledge that you already hold. In this case, to know your worth, you need to internalize the statements I've made above. Start by knowing that you deserve to be mad about it. You deserve to be angry with those who abandoned you. But you won't find your caregiver in other people. I could tell you that you have the right to exist, and by virtue of that, you deserve to have all your needs met. I could tell you that you do not have to perform for love, I could tell you that you don't need them to fill that void within you. They can't. But I know that it won't be that easy to believe me. You have learned to hide your sensitivity and vulnerability from the world because the gravity of allowing yourself to sink into these states of being feels threatening. You risk being alone. But if you want this wound to get better, and if you want healthy relationships, you have to be okay with being alone sometimes. Among other things and places, this is also where you get to know—and continue the work of grounding—yourself.

When you look inwards to finally tend to your abandonment wound, be prepared to accept that, while others in your life have failed you, you have also been your own worst enemy. Be prepared to take accountability for your own self-sabotage, and face the enemy within.

2: Abandonment Wounds Can Be Quite Complex.

Cuppen (2019) states that healing an abandonment wound can be a life-long journey if you keep at it. What might help is distinguishing between two kinds of respect: Treating a person as an authoritative figure, and treating someone as a person. The former only allows you a two-dimensional view of the person in question. When you treat someone—anyone—as an authority figure, you may feel you are not meant to question anything about them even in the face of disrespect. Viewing a person this way restricts you from being curious about who they are, and it often leads to you making excuses for them when they are meant to be held accountable. According to them, they "have their reasons." The latter form of respect widens your perspective and allows room for you to capture their mistakes and qualities as a part of their humanness. Viewing people this way sort of "levels the playing field," because you reach the inevitable understanding that you are all different, and that is what makes you all equal regardless of these differences. The former view of respect is likely how people with abandonment and people-pleasing issues were raised to perceive their caregivers. Authoritative respect often extends outside of parental relationships, to other authority figures, peers, and even those younger than themselves. Moreover, the people who were raised this way are hardly ever aware that they view everyone in their lives from a place of respecting them as authority figures. Apart from abandonment and people-pleasing tendencies, perhaps this is another facet of what drives passive-aggressiveness and victim mentality. This may be another reason why people with abandonment wounds find themselves in imbalanced co-dependent relationships.

Like people-pleasing, part of healing your abandonment is accepting that you played a part in your own emotional demise, as a result of loneliness, self-loathing, or "victim mentality." Kets de Vries (2012) describes people with a victim mentality as passive-aggressive in their interactions with others. Being passive-aggressive allows them to be very subtle, indirect, in order to get what they want and express their anger or displeasure without openly acknowledging it, or directly confronting the source of it. With an unhealed abandonment wound, from time to time, you will feel too angry to stay quiet about it. However, because you are too afraid to directly voice out your emotions, being passive-aggressive is the only way you feel safe. When you express yourself so as not to risk upsetting the other person so much that they might just walk out on you, triggering your abandonment trauma. It is also manipulative. Ultimately, your intention is to make the other person feel bad or to make them think that they are not doing enough to make you feel good about yourself. You may use the passive-aggressive style of interaction when you want to get what you want, even at the expense of the other person, for the same reasons. Your victim mentality will enable you to justify your manipulative actions because how could anyone not know how you feel or what you want when they should be paying all their attention to you all the time?

Your actions, and perhaps even your intentions, may be understandable but they can't be absolved on account of your emotions and your unmet (and unexpressed needs). Be upfront about what you want and how you feel, the worst that could happen is you face rejection. Understand that being rejected says more about the person who did it than it ever will about you. The irony of carrying unresolved abandonment trauma is that the coping mechanisms you develop as a means for your survival in what feels like an unsafe environment end up trapping you in unhealthy cycles of living, mentally, emotionally, physically, and if you believe in it, spiritually. Kets de Vries (2012) notes that people who are passive-aggressive have a "blame game repertoire," and the truth is it makes sense to blame the world for not providing a space where you learned how to deal with yourself. But you're growing up now, it's not their responsibility anymore. It's yours.

Chapter 3:

Jealousy

What a frowned-upon emotion. I believe that emotions are states of being that can be pleasant or unpleasant. Whether or not they feel good does not imply that they are inherently good or bad. We are far too complex as humans to dumb down our internal experiences into neat binaries. We need to be willing to acknowledge and accept that we can exist on both spectrums of 'good' or 'bad' feeling emotions. Like grieving for your loved one while still being able to appreciate humor, or being upset with your friend for ruining your favorite piece of clothing while being utterly shocked and slightly amused by how dumb they acted. Jealousy is an emotion like any other; it needs to be felt and addressed. While it may be triggered by external factors or situations, it is only entirely indicative of some part of you that needs to be tended to. It doesn't mean that you have to deal with it alone, it's almost impossible to fully address something within you without some degree of unwavering and honest support. However, you do need to take full accountability for choosing to deal with it however you see fit.

Yong and Li (2018) have noted that plenty of research has been invested into the idea of jealousy, considering its running theme in religious parables (such as Cain and Abel in the bible) and folklore (The Cherokee Sun

Myth), as well as modern television (*Twilight* movie series). Thinkers have deemed it as a psychological illness, others have deemed it an inferior part of humanity that needs to be thwarted or should not exist. What they have all noted, however, is that feelings of jealousy often arise when there is "a threat of a valued relationship being usurped by a third party." Yong and Li (2018) have have also noted that jealousy is "a troublesome emotional experience" that often causes misery and leads to those afflicted by it to turn to unwise coping mechanisms, such as stalking or violent aggression. However, they also argued that as opposed to jealousy being deemed 'poisonous' or 'toxic' in other studies, this emotion plays a significant role in our lives. But first, let's talk about the 'ugly' side of jealousy.

As Yong and Li (2018) have noted, jealousy arises when you feel that you might lose someone you value to someone else that you feel is better than you somehow, and therefore this presents competition to you. They further state that jealousy is often characterized by a social triangle. This could be your friend meeting new people and spending time with them, your partner or lover also meeting new people, even your parents, finding new partners in the event of a separation. In either situation, you feel threatened by the new third parties because your expectations of the relationship being exclusive have been violated (Yong and Li, 2018, p. 2). Whenever your valued person spends time with them, it upsets you because, in your mind, they are gaining the upper hand in this competition you feel you're in. If you struggle to express yourself, you revert to being passive-aggressive, which may be detrimental to your valued relationship in the long run. There is this popular misconception that when you "act jealous," then it means you care. While that may be true, it's not the whole story. Your valued person is exactly: A person, like yourself. You and your valued person will always meet other people and find some kind of interest in each other, and whether or not you are in an exclusive relationship, this is out of your control. When you allow yourself to rationalize the situation, it makes sense, and yet it upsets you. Perhaps your valued person is spending more time with their new acquaintance, and no longer makes as much time for you. It's only right that this makes you sad. But they won't know unless you bring it up. Asking your valued person to stop seeing their new acquaintance might remedy how threatened you feel but that's only dealing with the outcome of your jealousy, not the cause. However, going with this solution is only a temporary fix because, as aforementioned, meeting new people and becoming a part of each other's lives is inevitable even for you. It's also not fair to ask your valued person, or anyone, to thwart an inborn trait and need that we all carry: Human interaction. However, if the thought of your valued person making time for someone new in their lives triggers thoughts like "Maybe I'm just not worth their time anymore," or "What do they have, that I don't?" or "He/She's trying to take (your valued person) away from me" or "Why can't (your valued person) talk about me like that?" or "Why can't you joke with me like that?" then it may be time for some deep introspection.

Yong and Li (2018) propose that jealousy serves a function that is significant to how we adapt in certain situations such as our "vigilance in protecting the relationships that matter to us." They have also noted that in a "triangle of relations" where feelings of jealousy arise, we may be reminded of how much we value certain relationships, especially if we had begun to take them for granted. However, jealousy still has a bad name because the negative outcomes it has elicited heavily outweigh the good. Yong and Li's (2018) proposition, however, seems to ring true. When you feel angry, it can indicate that your trust or values have been violated or something very personal to you has been treated with disrespect. Your responsibility at that moment—should it be safe—is to make it known that you are angry and why. You make the effort to address how you feel with whoever caused you to feel this way. Your anger acts as a protective barrier or boundary marker to either avoid situations that violate your values and/or be prompted to do something about them should they arise. Interestingly, your anger is also how you get to know yourself deeply. It acts as a solid part of your foundation for your values. For example, if you value justice, it will anger you if a teenage child's molester is not convicted with any jail time, or worse if they go free. Or something as simple as your morning ritual being interrupted because the fact that you have one implies that how you start your day is important to you. When we allow ourselves to be angry and loud about it, we set ourselves apart from everyone else by making clear what matters to us and what makes us uncomfortable. We can look at jealousy in the same way we look at anger (which is also associated with jealousy).

In a "triangle of relations," where feelings of jealousy (outrage, fear, sadness, humiliation, and embarrassment) arise, we often associate those feelings with the third party butting into what you assumed would be an 'exclusive' relationship. When you make that association, it's often a result of comparing yourselves to the third parties, looking at what you think is more attractive about them than it is about you. You might try to convince yourself that you're the one who is in turn better than them, going as far as stalking their social media or undermining them when they talk. This might make you feel better about yourself, but you might not stop feeling jealous either way. You could even say that the only reason why you make those comparisons is that you already believe that you're inadequate, whether you're aware of that belief or not. This is when you really need to dig deep and figure out the source of your jealousy, and this is when Yong and Li's proposition of jealousy's functionality comes in.

Yong and Li (2018) suggest that jealousy is an inherited part of our biological and psychological make-up. They reference the American geneticist Theodosius Dobzhansky's (1973) argument stating the complexities of our minds will be difficult to grasp without understanding what it was designed to do. To put this into perspective, they made an example of the way our generation loves protein, sugar, and fat which suggests that ripe fruit and meat were scarce and valued resources. In the same way, the powerful emotional experience of jealousy suggests that losing your mate to another causes pernicious adaptive problems, such as not being able to reproduce or simply not being able to survive alone. The benefits of having that mate have been usurped by another, and this may have led to drastic measures being taken to ensure that wouldn't happen. While this may no longer be our reality, this experience is suggested to have evolutionarily shaped the way we deal with perceived threats to what and who we are protective of. This proposition may also shed light on the idea of obsessive possessiveness. However, this biological trait may have never stopped evolving, if we apply it contextually to our time period. We no longer have to scour for resources, which—over time, with the evolution of society, and the conditions created that have been a breeding ground for "maladaptive jealousy"—has left us with a lot of internal work that we still struggle with. Thinking about your jealousy today may be an indication of a part of you that has been neglected either by you or your caregivers, or that there is a need of yours that has gone unmet. We've established that you are responsible for making your needs known, however, maybe all you need is reassurance from your friend, your partner, or your parents. There are ways in which this can go wrong, and we'll get to that in the next few paragraphs. Sometimes reassurance can only do so much in remedying your jealousy, depending on which end of the spectrum you're feeling it. Finding the root source of your jealousy is the key to having a deeper understanding of yourself and your needs. However, embarking on that journey may trigger some unresolved trauma that you may have acquired growing up or even as an adult navigating your own independent relationships. Be curious and courageous enough to figure out why you have buried feelings of inadequacy.

Jealousy is nothing to be embarrassed about, and neither is it something to be proud of. Figuring out the 'why' behind this emotional experience is only the beginning of understanding your deeper needs, expressing them may be the next step, and then there's working through it. There are people who have found themselves in situations where their jealousy is used against them or they are left alone in moments where they need to be reassured. When your valued person uses your jealousy against you, it may be their way of testing how loyal you are to them or how far you're willing to go in proving how strong your feelings are for them. It becomes a situation where your toxic coping mechanisms are triggered and they get the better of both of you, jeopardizing the relationship. If the third party is relishing the toxicity elicited by their presence in your relationship, and your valued person continuously ignores your feelings, it may be time to reevaluate the significance of that relationship.

What Do We Do About It?

1: Investigate It.

Accept that you are feeling this way and investigate the source. Often when jealousy arises, you'll find that it's your insecurities surfacing and asking for your attention. For example, if you're in the presence of the third (rival) party, you find yourself overcompensating for what you perceive as your inadequacies, answering questions that were not even asked because you feel intimidated. Your immediate reaction to being intimidated might be setting standards that are higher and more unattainable than the ones you've already set. It's a form of self-sabotage that will affect your relationship in the long run if your feelings are left unresolved. Your insecurities tend to stem from deep fears that you are unworthy of love or affection. Chung and Harris (2018) noted that it has been argued that fears of unworthiness can stem from how quickly, and consistently, one's needs were tended in infancy. The measure of how well and quickly an infant's needs are attended to forms a foundation on which "the infant develops its beliefs about what to expect from others as well as expectations of self." What's also worth mentioning is that one of the coping mechanisms of jealousy is fantasizing about the demise of your valued person's new relationship where you're the one who reveals the rival's true colors, causing your valued person to end the new relationship. Don't try to coddle yourself by telling yourself that your jealousy only means that you care. Possessiveness only means that you are not secure enough in your sense of self that you rely on your valued person to provide that security for you, which is risky and unfair. So start there.

Start by investigating how secure you are in your sense of self, investigate how much of your worth is reliant on how your partner treats you. Be mindful that doing this may trigger unresolved abandonment wounds, so tread lightly and reserve plenty of compassion for yourself. This doesn't mean that you have to be completely reliant on yourself for how you measure your worth. The truth is that your personal relationships will always affect how you view yourself because they are an intricate part of your experience of the world. However, there needs to be a balance, and you have a responsibility to maintain that balance. You need to be aware of its stability, and check in on it from time to time. Your valued persons are also in the same position, which means they also play a role in maintaining the balance. When your relationship is healthy, it will feel like more than just an exchange of reassurances. When your relationship isn't healthy, and the need for reassurance is burdensome, then you may need to reevaluate the significance of the relationship.

2: You're not Them, and You Never Will Be.

You will never be everything to your valued person. You have to trust that they have in your life because they want you in it, but you're one person and you can only offer and give so much. This is why each of us needs to establish healthy social lives. As aforementioned, we are part of each other's world experience. Let's bring back the "I have to"-basis from Chapter 1, where I stated that you need to think of the "I have to"-basis as a parameter in your mind, and you can switch it on or off based on how it affects your priorities first. In order for it to be effective, you need to know that you don't *have* to subscribe to other people's needs all the time, or to limiting beliefs. Acquire this 'parameter' and apply it to when feelings of jealousy arise. Know that—unless you've been taking your relationship for granted—you don't have to try to outdo your valued person's new relationship, nor do you need to view it as a competition. Respect its existence and gracefully allow room for it to grow without interfering. This doesn't mean that you have to like this new person, but you are responsible for being a decent human being by acknowledging and respecting them—especially if it matters to your person.

There is a certain liberation that comes with internalizing the fact that there isn't—nor will there ever be—another you in the world. It absolves you from trying to be anything but. It allows you to build a solid and secure base for your sense of self and your self-worth. It becomes easier to *own* who you are. It takes time, but the progress is rewarding. Admit to your insecurities, admit that you're fearful, admit that you're jealous, accept your weaknesses and try to understand them. Be brutally honest with yourself, but leave plenty of room for compassion towards yourself. You have that much capacity within yourself and more. Allow it. Strive for secure self-worth and expect that it will be rocked from time to time because it won't be perfect. Striving for perfection when it comes to reworking your internal wiring implies that there is a point where you can say you're finished, and maybe you'll feel that you have. But the reality is that when we're curious enough about ourselves—and we try to make sense of what we find—we often leave with answers but also with just as many questions, if not more. I think most people are afraid of that, and it contributes to them remaining in toxic cycles. We're afraid of finding out who we are because we fear the truth might just confirm how little we think of ourselves. Staying grounded in the truth you define for yourself is what helps us mediate the fear of the unknown because it will never be the same as anyone else's. It will only ever belong to you.

Chapter 4:

Relationship Anxiety

Let's take people-pleasing, fear of abandonment, and jealousy—discussed in the previous chapters—into account as we expand on the concept of relationship anxiety. The world we're growing up in has developed the habit of either romanticizing or frowning upon these traits in the people who exhibit them. This is understandable as they often elicit unfavorable outcomes. Whenever something poses a threat or may elicit unwanted outcomes, the immediate response is often to find an immediate solution. For example, coming across a large cockroach in the living room. Your first thought is to either get the bug spray from the kitchen or to grab the closest shoe to kill it immediately before it spreads its wings and starts its reign of terror in the house. The mistake we often make is applying that same logic when we feel intense and overwhelming emotions or situations. We feel terrified and we want that feeling to leave our bodies immediately, so we either suppress or cope in temporary or unhealthy ways. Emotional wounds are exactly like physical wounds, they need to be tended to with patience and care, especially when they need to be rubbed with alcohol (brutal honesty) or develop an infection. If the wound is not tended to at all or if it is remedied recklessly, the infection may worsen and spread (unresolved trauma causing a rift in relationships). When emotional wounds are left unresolved, the behaviors they produce subconsciously extend into all other interpersonal relationships, which may then lead to relationship anxiety. Unresolved traumas stunt the development of our emotional intelligence, they make us afraid because being ourselves has left us feeling alone and unwanted, so much that we're often confused about how we *should* be. We become extremely mindful of our external environment to make sure that it doesn't trigger those wounds.

Hermes (2018) notes that the overall functioning of an individual is linked to the quality of the relationships that they are involved in. She has argued that mindfulness "exerts a significant influence on relationship quality for both individuals and their partners and is thus an important point of intervention for maximizing relationship functioning." Hermes' (2018) argument implies that paying attention to your valued person's personality traits and treating them based on which traits bring out the best (and the worst) in them heavily impacts the quality of the relationship, as well as the quality of your (and their) well-being. So what happens when one person in the relationship withdraws their mindfulness? How does the imbalance that follows impact both of them?

The reality of growing up today is that the world— consciously and subconsciously—perceives heteronormative narratives—whether in mainstream media or in ordinary conversations—as paramount. There is barely any space gracefully made for anything other than heteronormative narratives, and binary gender roles are enforced and imposed. You might grow up feeling different and displaced because you can't fit neatly into one gender role, and because there is no room for discussing anything different, you don't have the language to describe what you're going through. Alternatively, it might not bother you all that much and you seem to be able to adapt to the heterosexual narrative, but you're not part of it. Eventually, you meet someone that turns everything around, someone of the same sex as you, and someone you just happen to be attracted to. Now, considering that you may have/or struggle with the traits discussed in the previous chapters, your anxiety may begin to flare up within this new experience. You begin to realize that a lot of what you thought you knew did not apply to you at all, especially with regards to the heterosexual narrative. You begin to experience actual attraction for the first time, and scares you so much that it overwhelms you because you feel helpless. You've never had to deal with this before, and immediately, you'll feel the inordinate need to get everything right. In your mind, you see a stark difference between how to love the opposite sex of people and how to love the same sex, and you realize that you don't know how to romantically love someone of the same sex as you. This realization produces paralyzing fear, and you begin to experience relationship anxiety. (However, it also opens up the opportunity for you to explore uncharted territory in who you are.) You might begin to pay extreme attention to your valued person in order to understand every little thing about them, and this becomes your coping mechanism because it makes you feel safe. You believe it keeps you from ever making a mistake that will make your valued person think you're not good enough for them any longer, causing them to leave you.

Carporuscio (2020) notes that people—although interpersonal relationships are primarily a source of comfort and pleasure—worry about acceptance and reciprocal feelings from their valued persons. While this is normal to a certain degree, others develop anxiety and worry excessively about the future of their relationship. Due to this anxiety, they may end the relationship prematurely or stay in it while they endure the anxiety for the rest of its duration. Chung and Harris (2018) attribute this behavior to the "anxious attachment style," and as a result, the person with this attachment style will keep their feelings of inadequacy to themselves. To further this argument, Carporuscio (2020) states that when people experience relationship anxiety, they fear their efforts receiving poor evaluation and not being accepted. The problem with this mindset is that you are the one deciding for your valued person that you're not good enough for them. Your limiting beliefs about yourself will cause a dent in your valued relationships. They will cause you to withdraw, causing an imbalance in the relationship that will affect both of you.

Carporuscio (2020) notes that when people experience relationship anxiety, they need excessive reassurance, they self-silence, and they make accommodations for their partners at their own expense. Notice how the traits previously discussed seem to overlap when it comes to navigating our own relationships. Self-silencing may also be a result of developing an anxious attachment style. Having grown up in a home where self-silencing was the only way you could feel safe and receive affection, in your own interpersonal relationships, you may feel that this is how you get your needs met. While security and affection may be your primary needs in a relationship, they are not your only needs. Self-silencing is another self-sabotage coping mechanism because you hinder your growth as an individual on account of another. You betray yourself in order to have your primary needs met, the same way you had to, growing up. The difference now is that you're not dealing with someone who taught you to treat them solely as an authority figure, because even if you are, that person is your equal. The same goes for partner accommodation, which Carporuscio (2020) notes, is "observed as a response from the other partner towards the anxious partner." When we haven't learned to communicate effectively, we force the ones we love into positions where they are constantly trying to read between the lines, and this is exhausting. We force them into positions where they are vulnerable to manipulation, and not just from ourselves, whether we're aware of it or not. Carporuscio (2020) states that excessive reassurance-seeking is related to codependency, as it eventually becomes burdensome on your valued relationship. To add to this argument, when one partner exhibits relationship anxiety, and the other feels forced to make accommodations for them then we may conclude that relationship anxiety can be a breeding ground for ruinous codependency.

Relationship anxiety is ultimately a response to feeling powerless or helpless in the relationships that matter to you, but this helplessness is not triggered by external factors like your valued people. It's triggered by your limiting beliefs, fears, and insecurities. It's also triggered when a part of you that you had never been aware of reveals itself suddenly, messing with the impression you've already established in your relationships. This also makes you feel powerless because of the way this new trait creeps up on you and you have no idea how to navigate it. It scares you.

What Do We Do About It?

1: Allow It, Acknowledge It.

More often than not, the helplessness we feel when we experience relationship anxiety is perpetuated by our own unwillingness to allow ourselves to be present at the moment. We worry too much about what might happen next, and about finding a fix. Allow the anxiety to play out in your mind and sift out the loudest thoughts that arise from it. To allow is not synonymous with "giving in" to the anxiety as that would be risky and exacerbate what could already be a debilitating experience. Allow the thoughts to show up in your mind, because suppressing the thoughts may cause them to re-occur more rigorously at a later stage. Be present with them, acknowledge them without judgment. Relationship anxiety often creates the illusion of control that we desperately try to grab onto as the relationship progresses. You begin to invest in the relationship from an unrequited point-of-view even with a supportive partner, friend, or parent. Raypole

(2019) states that perhaps this relationship will end in a few months or years, but it doesn't mean that you can't enjoy it in the meantime. Therefore, what may also help to keep you present and grounded is to "prioritize your day-to-day experiences with your valued person," even the ordinary and mundane ones (Raypole, 2019). Perhaps what is also worth mentioning is the misconception that even if you are aware of your internal wounds, you need to have worked on them to a satisfactory extent before you are ready to be loved. This reinforces the belief that we need to perform for affection and love, and consequently fuels the relationship anxiety. The truth of this matter is that working on internal wounds can be a lifelong process (Cuppen, 2019). It is—at worst—inhumane to require someone to perform for your love and affection. Essentially, when unmet needs become unmet expectations, leading to passive-aggressiveness—this is what we are subjecting our loved ones to, even if we're acting from a place of hurt.

Raypole (2019) notes that unless the anxiety is caused by something specific—like your valued person prioritizing work over spending quality time with you—it often has nothing to do with your partner. It is, however, indicative of your internal issues being triggered and calling for your attention, causing an eruption of emotions. Treat this eruption the same way you would treat your thoughts. Breathe, and allow them to surface. When they do surface, try not to act on them as this may lead to impulsive and regretful outcomes (Raypole, 2019). The future of your relationship is not up to you alone, and you need to work on accepting that this is an inevitable fact. Try not to look at it from a restrictive point of view, but a liberating one. Yes, relationships take work, but it shouldn't feel like self-inflicted torture.

Valuing your relationships—with others and yourself—and your well-being means going through the discomfort of your internal muck in order to maintain their stability and quality. However, you can't identify solely with the stability and quality of your relationships. You need to continually build and remove and maintain your identity. Raypole (2019) argues that as your relationships deepen, you might find that certain parts of your identity—and your independence—begin to shift to make room for your valued person and the relationship itself. Hence, it remains paramount that, regardless of this shift, you maintain your identity (Raypole, 2019). Your individuality is most likely what brought them closer to you, so pushing the intricate parts of it down might only cause a rift between you, yourself, and your valued person.

2: Practice and Maintain Good Communication.

Say what you mean, and mean what you say, always. Considering the traits discussed in the previous chapter, this would be easier said than done as confrontation may not be a strong point for you here. Having had an experience that left you with internal wounds such as the fear of abandonment or fear of attachment—or especially having grown up with a weak establishment of trust—you might not have the language to express yourself in a way that satisfies your need to express how you feel or what you're going through. It's likely that you were only taught to express your physical needs, like hunger or fatigue, but you may be timid even when you communicate those needs. Raypole (2019) argues that using "I-statements" may help. Personalize your feelings and needs so they feel like they belong to you, and that they're not these burdens triggered by external factors. For example:

"I feel neglected when you spend an entire day without talking to me. I understand that your day gets busy, mine does too. I would like you to communicate with me if you're going to have a busy day so I know to only text or call you at the end of the day. I don't appreciate feeling like I need to pester you during the day just to hear how you're doing. It matters to me, you know."

Here, you have clearly expressed how you feel and you have communicated your needs to your valued person. Still, this might be difficult for someone with anxiety. If you struggle with face-to-face confrontation as a result of anxiety, then perhaps this is the first thing you need to communicate with your valued person. If they care about you—and if they haven't given you a reason to feel unsafe when you communicate with them—they will listen to you with patience and compassion. Consider the "letter method" as your mode of communication while you work your way up to face-to-face confrontation. The letter method, as the term suggests, is writing a letter to your valued person expressing your feelings and needs. You can ask them to either write back to you, or to respond to you in a conversation that you set time aside for. This mode of communication is just as respectable as an in-person conversation.

In the event of an argument, your anxiety might flare up, triggering your fight-or-flight or freeze response. Ultimately, you won't be able to respond constructively in the conversation. You might shut down and withdraw within yourself because in that moment, your anxiety convinces you that your worst fears about the relationship are about to be realized. You might self-silence for the exact same reasons. Know that it's okay to pause so you can recollect, and bring yourself back. Unless your valued person explicitly voices that they're leaving you, then you have no reason to believe that they will. Stay present in what is happening between you presently. You could even ask to 'table' the conversation for a later time in the day or the following day. Whatever is causing the conflict is not worth an escalated argument that may deal some irreparable damage, and it doesn't have to be resolved immediately. Take your time with each other. You can also table a conversation in the event that it reveals something that needs your introspection. As we become closer with our valued people, we begin to learn more about ourselves through our bond with them. Sometimes we like what we find, and sometimes we don't, especially if it doesn't align with who we want to be or who we see ourselves to be. We then have a responsibility to try and make sense of whatever was revealed in relation to ourselves and the relationship, and to loop our valued people from time to time about our progress.

Raypole (2019) notes that while telling your partner about your anxiety regarding the relationship might not alleviate it, looping them in might help them be more mindful within the relationship. Be careful not to put yourself or your valued person on a pedestal. Remember that you are equals in your relationship. When either of you put each other on a pedestal, it stunts the development of your communication and your bond because, as someone who experiences relationship anxiety, you might accept your valued person's opinion too easily without assessing how much it actually resonates with you. If you start acting out, your valued person might feel like they have to make accommodations for you (because they 'understand' you) even if it is at their expense. This is another reason why you need to be secure in your identity, as well as why it's important to be aware of each other's internal experiences; through communication.

Conclusion

And so we've come full circle once again.

Whether you've broken your circle or not at this point will never be a train smash, but be proud. Heck, *I'm* proud of you! I will keep reminding you, so you keep reminding yourself: Reworking your internal wiring is a continuous process that may take your entire lifetime. However, you will notice that as you keep it, you gain more and more control as your sense of self-awareness becomes clearer and clearer. You will feel more secure in your identity, allowing it to be more fluid as it is no longer anchored by anything outside of you. However, be careful not to get addicted to this process. You don't need to work on yourself every day, so try not to turn it into another coping mechanism. Rushing this process also implies—again—that there is a point of completion. Perhaps you do reach a point where you have eradicated some of your toxic traits or states of being, depending on the level of complexity they constituted. However, the reality of being human is that you can never know enough about yourself, not when nothing about the world is set in stone. Evolution never stops, and it goes without saying that this applies to us as well. Healing is not a neat and linear experience, nothing about being human is. Healing is messy, expect that. Expect that you won't feel rooted in anything for however long a while. Expect the confusion and the frustration. Expect, not just the discomfort of your emotions, but also the pain, the resentment, and the anger. Expect that your people-pleasing tendencies will only gradually fall away. Expect your body to tremble and convulse as you release your audible cries, and relish the brief bliss that comes when that burning lump in your chest is suddenly gone. Align your healing with whatever you believe in if you are a believer. It will strengthen your support system and your sense of security in self.

Everything is contextual. Applying what we learn about ourselves won't always be a straightforward process because there are situations we can never think to find ourselves in until we do. How we react in these situations can be informed by what we know now, or by our past mindsets, even if we've come a long way in our recovery. If it is the latter reaction that is triggered, then we need to remember that the body has a logic of its own (Oyěwùmí, 2005), and we won't always understand nor will we be aware of this logic. When we need to use our motor functions (walking, typing, swimming, etc.), our brains send messages throughout the different mechanisms of the body to make this possible. When we see a threat from afar, our bodies respond to the fear and alertness that arises. That fear is stored in our sense memory. Imagine washing the dishes in your kitchen, and all you're focusing on is that task in front of you. Suddenly you feel a cool metal instrument land gently on the base of your neck. Your body might shudder or freeze in fear before your brain processes that it's the bore of a gun. Your body remembers being in danger before you do, it reminds you through your senses being heightened. In the same way, when we become familiar with feeling unsafe at a young age, or through a traumatic experience in adulthood, our bodies remember those experiences and archive them. When we face situations that trigger feelings of unsafety, our bodies remind us as a means to warn and protect us from the perceived danger, such as being abandoned or watching a valued person form new relationships with other people. Sometimes our reactions to situations similar to the ones that caused the trauma can be automatic, and even embarrassing. However, subconscious actions are something to keep in mind in your healing process. Part of the process of healing is allowing ourselves to feel where the trauma sits in our bodies and finding ways to release it. The longer you practice staying grounded, the easier it will be to stay present at the moment and to pay attention to the things you do subconsciously.

Your coping mechanisms will also fall away gradually, the more you become aware of them, both conscious and subconscious. People often make the mistake of setting the end goal as the first step in their recovery. For example, if they want to stop smoking, they do so abruptly, from smoking a pack or two a day to none. Perhaps this is part of the reason why relapsing is likely during a person's recovery from addiction. Learned habits such as smoking or people-pleasing need to be given as much effort and time it took to acquire them. If you resolve abrupt solutions, the mind and body alike will protest at this sudden change. It won't be appreciated, and unless you have strict and untethered dedication towards your abrupt goal, it may also be a losing battle. Therefore, set realistic and strategic goals. For example, if you smoked two packs of cigarettes a day, take it down to one for a week or two. After that set period, try not to finish a pack in one day for another week or two, and so on. In the meantime, find new hobbies to distract yourself from the urge to smoke relentlessly, develop healthy eating habits if you haven't already. Strategize however you see fit and commit to that strategy. As previously discussed, people-pleasing is one of the few ways an unhealed wound can overtly manifest. One of the steps to overcome people-pleasing habits discussed was that if you're too afraid to say "No," then start by stalling. Give yourself the permission to think about whether or not you want to agree to a request or an offer, because you have every right to. Stall for as long as you need to while you work up the courage to express your final decision. It is worth mentioning, however, that addiction is an illness that requires complex medical treatment, patience, and understanding. Recovery is hardly ever linear. People-pleasing habits may also be complicated, being deeply rooted in unrelenting fears.

You need to understand that you are not the best or worst parts of yourself, those are your attributes. Your people-pleasing tendencies or your fear of abandonment, your jealousy issues, and your relationship anxiety are enmeshed by-products of you learning to survive in an environment that was meant to be conducive for your healthy upbringing. It was how you felt safe, but it became more ruinous as you grew older. The thoughts that fuel these behaviors may have become a part of your daily thought patterns, repeating themselves every day to reinforce your insecurities. A trick I learned over time was to try not to react to those thoughts, and to ask myself how substantial those thoughts may be about me, or how someone else feels about me. A lot of the negative thought spirals we get caught up in are external opinions that we internalized when we still accepted them easily. Therefore, if you can't provide a logical reason for whatever is causing you to panic, then you have no reason to believe that it's real or true. For example, something as simple as your message not getting delivered (typically indicated by two ticks) or a response all day, might lead you to believe that they blocked you or they don't love you anymore. Since your thought pattern is constantly trying to come up with a reason to prove that your worst fears are coming true, you might begin to pick yourself apart, trying to figure out which part of you drove them away. All those thoughts are geared at reverting this imaginary blame onto you, and this consumes you. Even as these thoughts hurl at you, ask yourself if you really know the reason why they haven't gotten back to you. Your thoughts are just speculations! Unless they say it or do it explicitly, you have no reason to assume the worst.

Another thing we need to come to terms with is rejection, this inevitable thing we all go through at some point in our lives. People tend to minimize the effects of rejection, telling each other to just "get over it." As Cuppen (2019) has argued that people who live with the fear of abandonment or attachment—as well as those who exhibit the attributes previously discussed— develop an acute sensitivity, which means that the experiences that are considered normal for most people, are more difficult for them to process. Rejection is hard, even more so for acutely sensitive people. However, understanding that rejection is an indication of someone else's preferences may help in alleviating the grief it brings. Rejection never brings your worth into question. When the first thing you experience as you enter the world is some degree of rejection—other than developing a very deep fear 0f rejection (it's painful enough for you to understand that you need to avoid feeling it, it becomes a threat) or people-pleasing tendencies or relationship anxiety—you also experience grief. That grief accumulates as you grow older. Grief is the by-product of growing up with the responsibility of looking out for yourself before you had even developed your self-awareness. As you unearth the effects of the negligence (and even abuse) that you may have had to protect yourself from, you will also grieve the loss of your childhood. You will grieve the relationships that should have been your source of comfort and security. You will also grieve the relationships that could have been good for you when you expected the worst from them because trusting the compassion that might have been offered to you would have been in conflict with how you've had to live: through surviving. It will hurt, and you might be upset with yourself, but try not to be so hard. Acknowledge and accept the times when you didn't know any better.

I want to stress that as much as working on yourself is your responsibility, you do not have to go it alone. You might think so, but don't fall for that misconception. You don't have to show up to the world "fully healed," not when there are new people to meet and new love to experience. All of that will come with cherishable times, and hardships. Hardship is the one thing no human can escape, it's part of being secure in your identity. When you solidify your own personal values, it is guaranteed that they will be either directly or indirectly violated by a situation you are involved in or one that is outside of you. The irony of working through trauma is that even though you experienced it in old relationships, you also repair some of it within new relationships. There are parts of you that can only be revealed by the shift that a relationship causes in your life. The hardest part of it all is that you are teaching yourself all the things that the world expects you to have figured out by the time you are considered an adult. At the same time, you are learning how to be kind to yourself when it comes to your shortcomings. Learning to navigate relationships, identity, and even sexual orientation isn't part of the school curriculum, and these topics are not properly represented in mainstream media.

It may be safe to assume that there has hardly been any mainstream attention brought in to understand the mechanisms that drive these traits. Big companies now use mental health awareness as part of their marketing strategies to appeal to their audiences and increase sales. As anyone would expect, the campaigns only deal with surface-level mental health tips, not how to be mindful when interacting with people who struggle with mental illnesses or their mental health. It goes without saying that the general public needs to be aware of the internal issues that so many among us face, beyond just the surface level. However, the world seems to be gradually going in that direction, although there is much work left to be done.

I hope after all the work you've been doing on yourself, and the work you will continue doing has allowed you to breathe better, and to feel lighter. I hope you've learned to welcome love and compassion and to hold space for all good things within yourself. I hope you know that you deserve as many chances as you can give yourself to start over. I hope you learn to overcome the enemy within, and come out stronger, wiser, and welling with love. I hope you know that sometimes it takes surrendering to your emotions before you gain back control once more. If you've made it here to this point, again, I'm proud of you. I hope your circle has broken, and I hope it's wider.

References

Caporuscio, J. (2020, April 1). *Relationship anxiety: Signs, causes, and management.* Medical News Today. https://www.medicalnewstoday.com/articles/r elationship-anxiety

Carroll, D. A. (2007). *Psychology of Language* (5th ed.). Wadsworth Publishing.

Chung, M., & Harris, C. R. (2018). Jealousy as a Specific Emotion: The Dynamic Functional Model. *Emotions in Review,* 1(4). https://doi.org/DOI: 10.1177/1754073918795257

Cuppen, H. (2019). *Abandonment and intimacy A tension filled   dynamic.* https://www.hannahcuppen.nl/wp-content/uploads/2019/03/Article-Abandonment-and-Intimacy-a-thrilling-dynamic-Marc.pdf

Dobzhansky, T. (1973). Nothing in Biology Makes Sense except in the Light of Evolution. *The American Biology Teacher,* 35(3), 125–129. https://doi.org/10.2307/4444260

Fernandez, E. M., & Smith Cairns, H. (2018). *Language Acquisition*. Hunter College and the Graduate Center, City University of New York.

Hermes, C. C. (2018). *The influence of anxiety and mindfulness on relationship quality: An investigation of comparative and dyadic effects.* file:///C:/Users/Student/Documents/Work%20docs/Codependency%20Workbook%20order/Hermes_Thesis_Final%20Draft.pdf

Kets de Vries, M. F. R. (2012). Are You a Victim of the Victim Syndrome? *SSRN Electronic Journal,* 43(2), 130–137. https://doi.org/10.2139/ssrn.2116238

Martin, S. (2019). *Your guide to understanding people-pleasing & codependency what is people-pleasing?* http://sharonmartincounseling.com/wp-content/uploads/2016/09/Codependency-Guide.pdf

NAFSA. (2010, May 17). *Linguistic determinism linguistic relativism.* NAFSA. https://www.nafsa.org/professional-resources/browse-by-interest/linguistic-determinism-linguistic-relativism#:~:text=In%20everyday%20terms%2C%20we%20hear

Oyěwùmí, O. (2005). *African Gender Studies A Reader* (O. Oyěwùmí, Ed.). Palgrave Macmillan US. https://doi.org/10.1007/978-1-137-09009-6

Piaget, J. (1962). *Play, dreams, and imitation in childhood / Translated by C. Gattegne and F.M. Hodgson.* New York: W.W. Norton.

Raypole, C. (2019, November 14). *Relationship anxiety: 16 signs and tips.* Healthline. https://www.healthline.com/health/relationship-anxiety#overcoming-it

Yong, J. C., & Li, N. P. (2018). The Adaptive Functions of Jealousy. In *The Function of Emotions* (In: Lench, H. (eds), pp. 121–140). Springer, Cham. https://doi.org/10.1007/978-3-319-77619-4_7